Three foxes passed a bakery
while going to the fair.
Said the foxes to the baker,
"We'd like to taste your wares.

FAIR

1

They liked the tasty muffins
the very best of all.
They said, "Let's buy them for the fair —
we'll have a muffin stall."

Foxy Number One soon sold
her share to two small mice.
They said, "We'll buy all 24 —
they look so very nice!"

Foxy Number Two sold hers
to three big fluffy rabbits.
Muffins would be a special treat —
much tastier than carrots.

Four squirrels soon bought all the rest,
from Foxy Number Three.

Walking away each squirrel said,
"How many muffins for me?"

Good, we've got equal shares!

The squirrels all were happy
as they headed home that night.

Then they spied the rabbits and mice — and something didn't seem right.

It's not fair! That little mouse has got more than me.

So they split up the muffins again, and made it like a game.